KT-556-268

WITH ALL MY LOVE

JOHN
XXX
23-9-98

**Other giftbooks by Helen Exley:**
When Love is Forever
Missing You...

Published simultaneously in 1997 by Exley Publications in Great Britain,
and Exley Giftbooks in the USA.

12  11  10  9  8  7  6  5  4  3  2

Copyright © Helen Exley 1997

ISBN 1-85015-777-4

**Edited and pictures selected by Helen Exley.**

Designed by Pinpoint Design Company.
Pictures researched by P. A. Goldberg and J. M. Clift, Image Select, London.
Typeset by Delta, Watford.
Printed in Hungary.
Exley Publications Ltd, 16 Chalk Hill, Watford, Herts WD1 4BN, United Kingdom.
Exley Giftbooks, 232 Madison Avenue, Suite 1206, NY 10016, USA.

**Acknowledgements:** ALBAN BERG: Extracts from *Alban Berg: Letters to his Wife* ed. by
Evans, Bernard Grun. Reprinted by permission of Faber & Faber. GERALD BUNYAN:
Extract from *Forces Sweetheart*. Reprinted by permission of Bloomsbury Publishing Plc.
KAHLIL GIBRAN: Extract from *Gibran Love Letters*. Reprinted by permission of Alfred A.
Knopf and The National Committee of Gibran 1951. © All rights reserved. R. M. GOMM:
Extract from "This Morning" from *The Seasons of My Life*. Published by Mitre Press, 1973.
ANDREW HARVEY: Extract from "A Full Circle" © André Deutsch Ltd 1981. FRAN
LANDESMAN: Extract from "Wasted" from *More Truth Than Poetry*. Reprinted by
permission of Jay Landesman Ltd. OGDEN NASH: Extract from *Loving Letters from Ogden
Nash* © 1990 Isabel Nash Eberstadt & Linell Nash Smith. Reprinted by permission of Little
Brown & Co Ltd and Curtis Brown Ltd. WILLIAM PLOMER: Extract from "Visiting the
Caves". Reprinted by permission of Random House Ltd. ELIZABETH JENNINGS: Extract
from "Absence" from *Collected Poems*, Carcanet Press. Reprinted by permission of David
Higham Associates Ltd. CHIEN WEN TI: Extract from "Winter Night" translated by Arthur
Walley. Reprinted by permission of HarperCollins*Publishers*. PU SÜAN TSU: Extract from
*Further Collection of Chinese Lyrics* ed. Ayling & Mackintosh. Reprinted by permission of
Routledge. YEVGENY YEVTUSHENKO: Extract from "Incantation" from *Love Poems:
Gollancz Poets*. Translated by Stanley Kunitz with Anthony Kahn. Reprinted by permission of
Bantam Doubleday Dell Publishing Group, Inc. **Picture Credits:** Alinari (ALI), Art Resource
(AR), Artworks (AW), Bridgeman Art Library (BAL), Christie's Colour Library (CI),
Edimedia (EDM), Fine Art Photographic Library (FAP), Giraudon (GIR), Index (I), Scala
(SCA), Sotheby's Transparency Library (STL), Statenskonst Museer, Stockholm (SKM),
Superstock (SS), Tate Gallery (TG). Cover: © 1997 Carl Holsoe, Pouring Coffee in an
Interior, STL; title page: John Singer Sargent, AR; p.6: © 1997 Lionel Walden, Train at Night,
BAL; p.8/9: Alphonse Asselbergs, FAP; p.10/11: Lieff Kamenev, SCA; p.13: John Atkinson
Grimshaw, BAL; p.15: Jean Raoux, GIR/AR; p.17: © 1997 Juri Pimenov, The Rain Shower,
SCA; p.18/19: Walter Boodle, FAP; p.21: Umberto Boccioni, EAF, AL/AR; p.23: A.
Mortaratsch, SS; p.25: Vassili Sounikov, EDI; p.27: John Atkinson Grimshaw, BAL; p.29:
Henri de Toulouse-Lautrec, AR; p.31: Jacopino del Conte, SCA; p.32/33: E. Longoni, AL;
p.35: Claude Monet; p.37: Ivan Aivazovsky, SS; p.38/39: Dan Brown, AW; p.40: William
Stott, TG/AR; p.42: John Singer Sargent, BAL; p.44: © 1997 Peter Vilhelm Ilsted, A Girl
Seated in a Sunlit Room, STL; p.46: Pierre Prins, EDI; p.48: © 1997 Margaret Preston, Rock
Lily, BAL; p.51: Frans Timen, SKM; p.53: Paul Merwart, BAL; p.55: John William Godward,
BAL; p.56: Eugene Jansson, SKM; p.59: Joaquin Sorolla; p.61: Paul Paeschke, CI.

# THINKING
## of YOU

EDITED BY
HELEN EXLEY

EXLEY
NEW YORK • WATFORD, UK

*This is to let you know*
*That all that I feel for you*
*Can never wholly go.*
*I love you and miss you, even two hours away,*
*With all my heart. This is to let you know.*

NOEL COWARD (1899-1973)

*I find you in all small and lovely things; in the little fishes like flames in the green water, in the furred and stupid softness of bumble-bees fat as laughter, in all the chiming radiance of warmth and light and scent in the summer garden.... When a person that one loves is in the world and alive and well, and pleased to be in the world, then to miss them is only a new flavour, a salt sharpness in experience.*

WINIFRED HOLTBY (1898-1935)

LIVING HERE FAR AWAY
I AM YOURS
LIVING THERE FAR AWAY
YOU ARE MINE
LOVE IS NOT MADE
OF BODIES ONLY
DEEP IN THE HEARTS
IS WHERE WE ARE ONE.

SANSKRIT LOVE POETRY

In my imagination, on foggy mornings or
afternoons with the sun bouncing
off northwest water, I try to
think of where you might be in your life and
what you might be doing as
I'm thinking of you. Nothing complicated –
going out to your garden, sitting
on your front porch swing, standing at the
sink in your kitchen. Things like
that. I remember everything. How you
smelled, how you tasted like the
summer. The feel of your skin against mine,
and the sound of your
whispers as I loved you.

ROBERT JAMES WALLER,
FROM "THE BRIDGES OF
MADISON COUNTY"

I am just walking around here between
the lines [of my letter], under the light
of your eyes, in the breath of your
mouth as in a beautiful happy day.

FRANZ KAFKA (1883-1924),
FROM A LETTER TO MILENA JESENSKÁ

Your moorland strength
sustains me in the street,
And the thought of you
touches me
as a plectrum strings –
Child, parent, mate,
heart with a steady beat,
Yours is the warmth
in which the future sings.

WILLIAM PLOMER,
FROM "*VISITING THE CAVES*"

I live at the head of the Great River,
You live at the Great River's tail.
Daily I think of you; though I don't see you
Both of us drink from the Great River.

When will these waters fail?
When will these longings end?
I have one wish; that your heart and my heart
Stay true to love's bond.

P'U PU SUAN TZU, FROM *"FURTHER
COLLECTION OF CHINESE LYRICS"*

*I need your love*
*as a touchstone of my existence.*
*It is the sun*
*which breathes life into me.*
*I am going to bed.*
*I shall fall asleep*
*praying of you.*
*My need to see you happy*
*gives me faith.*
*My last waking thoughts,*
*and all my dreams,*
*are of you.*
*Juliette*

JULIETTE DROUET (1806-1883),
TO VICTOR HUGO

*I love the valleys in winter, Mary, when we sit by the fire, with the fragrance of burnt evergreen cypress filling the house and the snow falling outside, the wind blowing [it], the ice-lamps hanging outside the window-panes, and the distant sound of the river and the voice of the white storm uniting in our ears.*

*But if my little loved-one were not near me there would be no valley, no snow, no fragrance of cypress bough, no crystal lamps of ice, no river song, no awe-inspiring storm... Let all these things vanish if my blessed little one be far away from them and from me.*

KAHLIL GIBRAN (1883-1931) TO MARY HASKELL, FROM "*GIBRAN LOVE LETTERS*"

NEED: SOMETHING TO LIFT YOU FROM YOUR BOOTS
OUT INTO THE SKY, SOMETHING TO MAKE YOU LIKE
LITTLE THINGS AGAIN, TO WHIRL AROUND THE
CURVES OF YOUR EARS AND MUSS UP YOUR HAIR
AND CALL YOU EVERY DAY.

LORRIE MOORE, b.1957

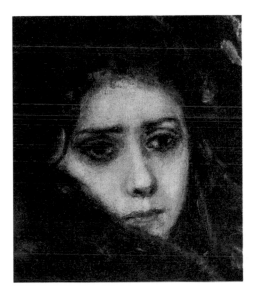

I ARISE FROM DREAMS OF THEE

IN THE FIRST SWEET SLEEP OF NIGHT,

WHEN THE WINDS ARE BREATHING LOW,

AND THE STARS ARE SHINING BRIGHT.

PERCY BYSSHE SHELLEY (1792-1822),
"THE INDIAN SERENADE"

## WINTER NIGHT

My bed is so empty
that I keep on waking up;
As the cold increases,
the night-wind begins to blow.
It rustles the curtains,
making a noise like the sea.
Oh that those were waves
which could carry me back to you!

CHIEN WĒN-TI

*As I sit here, I want you – I want you. I want to be at home with you. – anywhere. You're my country – my people – my whole life is bound up in yours. Come awfully close to me and let us hold each other tight a minute.*

*Ah, Love, Love, when I come back – we shall be so happy. The very cups and saucers will have wings and you will cut me the only piece of bread and jam in the world, and I will pour you out a cup of my tea. Why aren't you here, now, NOW. But I am coming, Bogey – and I am all your woman*

*Tig.*

KATHERINE MANSFIELD
(1888-1923),
FROM
"KATHERINE MANSFIELD'S
LETTERS TO JOHN
MIDDLETON MURRY 1913-1922"

I BESEECH YOU – IN THE STILLEST STILLNESS,

OR WHEN THE RAIN PATTERS ON YOUR ROOF,

OR THE SNOW SPARKS ON YOUR WINDOWPANES,

AND YOU LIE BETWEEN SLEEP AND WAKING –

THINK OF ME ON SPRING NIGHTS

AND THINK OF ME ON SUMMER NIGHTS,

THINK OF ME ON AUTUMN NIGHTS

AND THINK OF ME ON WINTER NIGHTS.

YEVGENY YEVTUSHENKO, b. 1933,
FROM "INCANTATION"

It was because
the place was just the same
That made your absence
seem a savage force,
For under all the gentleness
there came
An earthquake tremor:
fountain, birds and grass
Were shaken
by my thinking
of your name.

ELIZABETH JENNINGS, b.1926,
FROM *"ABSENCE"*

*My* adorable and beloved Frances –

*Seven* miles is not very far ordinarily, nor seven hours very long, but when they lie between us they seem multiplied by infinity. My heart is swollen with longing for you, and my mind is filled with your fragile and iridescent image. There is a silver echo of your voice in my ears, and my body tingles at the remembered flame of yours.

For some reason, God has seen fit to grant me the woman of all women, the always hitherto intangible, unattainable idea of every poet's dream and every man's desire. You are eternal youth and truth, tenderness and passion, and bright beauty that at once pierces and eases the heart. You are the vision that for a million years has drawn man up from the beast; and suddenly the vision is incarnate, and in my arms.

You are my light and air, my food and drink, my very inmost life.

I worship and adore you through all the eternities.

Ogden

OGDEN NASH (1902-1971),
TO FRANCES LEONARD, JULY 29, 1931

$\mathcal{H}$ave you really not noticed, then, that here of all places, in this private, personal solitude that surrounds me, I have turned to you? All the memories of my youth speak to me as I walk, just as the sea shells crunch under my feet on the beach. The crash of every wave awakens far-distant reverberations within me. I hear the rumble of bygone days, and in my mind the whole endless series of old passions surges forward like the billows. I remember my spasms, my sorrows, gusts of desire that whistled like the wind in the rigging, and vast vague longings that swirled in the dark like a flock of wild gulls in a storm cloud. On whom should I lean, if not you? My wary mind turns for refreshment to the thought of you as a dusty traveller might sink onto a soft and grassy bank.

GUSTAVE FLAUBERT (1821-1880)

The day is cold and dark.
The only ray that comes
to me, the sole source of
light and warmth, is my
memory of you, dear
Marie. I think back to our
awakenings in Como and
Florence... I feel I have
forgotten how to live.

FRANZ LISZT (1811-1886),
TO MARIE DE FLAVIGNY,
COMTESSE D'AGOULT

*When the redbird spread his sable wing,*
*And showed his side of flame;*
*When the rosebud ripened to the rose,*
*In both I read thy name.*

RALPH WALDO EMERSON (1803-1882),
FROM *"THINE EYES STILL SHINED"*

THE SUN CANNOT SHINE WITHOUT
YOU, THE BIRDS CAN MAKE NO MELODY.
THE FLOWERS HAVE NO OTHER BEAUTY
OR PERFUME — ALL IS A MEANINGLESS
WASTE. I LOVE YOU DARLING....
YOU ARE IN EVERY THOUGHT, DREAM,
HOPE, DESIRE.

AUSTIN DICKINSON (1829-1895),
LETTER TO MABEL TODD

# THIS MORNING

The sun must have climbed
round the edge of the window
this morning –
    caressing my face,
    and sleep filled eyes
    everso tenderly –

For,
    (in the fleeting
    wistful waking moments),
I thought
I prayed
that the gentle warmth
could be you...

R.M. GOMM,
FROM "THE SEASONS OF MY LIFE"

*... drenched,*

*and I am more than ever lost and lonely.*

*Oh love, dear love, behold me now without you,*

*The house, hungry for life, untenanted....*

OGDEN NASH (1902-1971)

# Wasted

Wasted are these days that I don't spend

    with you

Wasted are my empty nights

Wasted are these mornings and this

    postcard view

Wasted all the spring delights.

...

Wasted are the letters that I never send

Wasted are the poems I pen

Wasted my creations and my crazy dreams

Till I'm in your arms again.

FRAN LANDESMAN,
FROM "MORE TRUTH THAN POETRY"

*The birds have vanished into the sky,*

*and now the last cloud drains away.*

*We sit together, the mountain and me,*

*Until only the mountain remains.*

LI PO

## *Tristis eris si solus eris*
*(You will be sad if you are alone.)*

OVID (43 B.C.–18 A.D.)

*... it only dawned on me this evening that perhaps you will not be here again for a long time... that you won't see the dahlias of this year again reflected in your mirror and that the lemon verbena in a jar on my table will all be withered and dry.*

*As I thought that, sitting, smoking in the dusky room, Peter Wilkins [a black kitten] came in with a fallen-all-too-fallen leaf in his mouth, and I remembered that the Michaelmas daisies were out and, lo! it was autumn.*

KATHERINE MANSFIELD (1888-1923),
TO JOHN MIDDLETON MURRAY

Whatever I do, whichever way I turn, I see only,
I am reminded only, that I love you,
and I love you, and I love you. It's not just
simple idolatry. Of course it's instinctive, but
also I've reasoned it all out, in so far
as I can be at all reasonable about you. I've
compared your hair and your eyes
and your nose and your mouth and your figure
and your mind and your spirit and your whole
self with girls who are supposed to be
something oh very extra special – and always,
Frances, there's only you, all that's
darling and adorable, all that I've lived and
hoped for. Dearest, dearest, I'm not
really living when I'm away from you – only
hoping, and hope is so closely bound to fear!

OGDEN NASH (1902-1971),
IN A LETTER
TO FRANCES LEONARD,
SEPTEMBER 20, 1929

I am writing to you on Sunday evening, which is the time I like to write to you best, because I feel the quietest and descend the most into my real self, where my love is strongest and deepest. So you know I always have a fancy at such times that our love makes us somehow alone together in the world. We seem to have a deep life together apart from all other people on earth and which we cannot show, explain or impart to them. At least my affection seems to isolate me in the deepest moments from all others, and it makes me speak with my whole heart and soul to you and you only.

WALTER BAGEHOT
TO ELIZA WILSON, 1858

Across how many thousand miles
I lie
Tossing
To your heart beat.

ANDREW HARVEY,
FROM *"A FULL CIRCLE"*


Sweetheart, I am always with you –
do you feel my touch
In the quiet sometimes,
after the day is finished?

KENNETH HOPKINS,
EXTRACT FROM *"FROM A DISTANCE"*


Once again last night
you would not let me sleep.
Before I went to sleep
I moved over and made room for you
and tried to imagine you there
so soft and warm and smooth.

BOB GRAFTON,
TO HIS FUTURE WIFE DOT

My beloved girl,

It is nearly bedtime but I just couldn't turn in without saying "I love you". I love you until the wanting and desire of you, the ache in my heart, and the loneliness threaten to engulf me completely. Even in spite of the men around me, that loneliness is always there 'cos only you matter. I long so terribly to crush you into my arms and feel your body pressing closer and closer with each breath. Oh darling, I will go nuts if I don't see you soon 'cos the desire is nearly bursting me. I want to kiss your soft loveliness and feel your warm lips on mine as our bodies become one. Tonight there will be no you to caress, no dear breasts uplifting to my kisses, no scent of your hair – in fact, nothing at all. Your heart will be with me but my sleep will be empty, so different from the glorious contentment of having you beside me all the time. Please, I want so badly to be your real husband again and not just a bloke away from home whose heart is breaking to be with you.

... I want you. "Want" is such a big little word and you know all that it means to us.

GERALD BUNYAN, IN A LETTER TO HIS WIFE MAVIS, JULY 13, 1945

I shall always be near you;
in the gladdest days
and in the darkest nights...
always, always,
and if there be a soft breeze
upon your cheek,
it shall be my breath.

MAJOR SULLIVAN BALLOU,
TO HIS WIFE SARAH.

*I am always conscious
of my nearness to you,
your presence
never leaves me.*

JOHANN VON GOETHE (1749-1832),
TO CHARLOTTE VON STEIN

Darling, my darling, One line in haste to tell you
that I love you more today than ever in
my life before, that I never see beauty without
thinking of you or scent happiness without
thinking of you. You have fulfilled all my
ambition, realized all my hopes, made all my
dreams come true.
You have set a crown of roses on my youth
and fortified me against the disaster of our days.

DUFF COOPER

*I'm calm, in the certain knowledge that
nothing and nobody will sap our life,
and nothing – no cataclysm, no absence
– will wear down our love.*

SIMONE DE BEAUVOIR (1908-1986),
TO HER LIFETIME COMPANION JEAN-PAUL SARTRE